AND
FAMILY
PLANNING

A Christian
— View —

AIDS SEX AND FAMILY PLANNING

A Christian View

Dr KRISTINA BAKER
and HONOR WARD

Daughter of Honor Ward, whose husband was Professor Alan Ward, University of Ghana 1950 to 1962, Univ of Zambia 1962 →. She taught Felix Physics in Achimota.

AFRICA CHRISTIAN PRESS
ACHIMOTA, GHANA

© AFRICA CHRISTIAN PRESS

First published 1989

ISBN 9964 87 896 6

Quotations from the Bible are from the Revised Standard
Version. Copyrighted 1946 and 1952, unless otherwise
indicated.

Trade orders to:
Nigeria: Challenge Bookshops, PMB 12256, Lagos
and Fellent Ltd, PO Box 5923, Lagos
Zambia: ACP, PO Box 21689, Kitwe
Kenya: Keswick Bookshop, PO Box 10242, Nairobi
Zimbabwe: Word of Life Bookshops, PO Box 3700, Harare
South Africa: ACLA, PO Box 332, Roodepoort 1725,
Transvaal
Australia: Bookhouse, PO Box 115, Flemington Markets,
NSW 2129
UK: 50 Loxwood Avenue, Worthing, W. Sussex BN14 7RA

All other orders to:
Africa Christian Press, PO Box 30, Achimota, Ghana,
West Africa

Production and printing in Great Britain by
Nuprint Ltd, Harpenden, Herts AL5 4SE.

CONTENTS

1

The Doctor's surgery is in a small building in a side street, close to the centre of the big busy city. The Doctor working there is a man in his forties, who looks each patient straight in the face with a look which is both searching and compassionate. He was educated at a local High School and at the national University; he is an Elder of a local church; he is a man of that city; he knows its ways and its problems well. Under his white coat, in the breast-pocket of his cotton jacket, he carries a small pocket New Testament, and in the Testament, as a book-marker, is a small photograph of his wife; the Testament and the photograph are both very important to him.

The nurse who is working with the Doctor this morning has just called out the name 'Mrs Mkhwanazi'. Mrs Mkhwanazi is a woman of about forty years old, well dressed, but nervous and thin; she gets up from her seat in the waiting room, and moves into the surgery. She sits in the chair, looking at the doctor across the width of his desk, and twisting her hands together. After the usual greetings, the Doctor asks her, 'Now, what is the problem?'

'It's my son,' says Mrs Mkhwanazi. 'I'm worried about him, so terribly worried. He is a good boy, Doctor, I don't want you to think he would do bad things. He belongs to our church and sings in the choir, and he knows what is right. But now he has been given a place at the University, and he starts next week. There are so many bad people there, even some of the lecturers.'

'And are you afraid your son will get into bad habits?' the Doctor asked.

'Not really, Doctor. I told you, he is a good boy. But just last week one of the students from the University died of this thing, eh, what do you call it...?'

'You mean AIDS?'

'Yes, Doctor, AIDS. I'm afraid. I think we should keep him at home where he is safe and not let him mix up with these bad people who get these things. But he wants to go and my husband says we must let him; but he will be eating with these bad people, and washing with them; suppose he caught AIDS, and died? He is our only son, Doctor; we have three daughters, but only this one son.'

The Doctor looked very kindly at Mrs Mkhwanazi. 'I think I understand,' he said.

'He caught measles at school,' she went on. 'He went to boarding school because my husband said he had to go, but some of the boys had measles there, and he caught it and was very sick. I'm so afraid the same thing will happen again, and if he caught AIDS he would die. I'd rather he stayed at home with me.'

'I understand your fears,' said the Doctor. 'But I am sure you must let your son go to University. Now, let me explain.

'Measles is what we call an "infectious" disease. That means that if a boy or girl has measles, the measles virus particles – that's the tiny living things, like germs, which carry the infection – are in their throat and nose. When they cough or sneeze the virus particles escape into the air, and if other children breathe that air, some of the virus will go into their throat or their nose and they may well catch measles. We call it *droplet infection*, because the virus particles floating in the air are carried on tiny drops of water thrown out with the cough or the sneeze. That's why we tell people with a bad cold, or with measles, to use a handkerchief; it helps to trap the droplets.

'Now, Mrs Mkhwanazi, do believe me, AIDS is completely different. It is impossible to catch the AIDS virus by sitting near someone who has AIDS, and breathing the air they breathe. Even if you share a hand towel, or use the same lavatory, or eat at the same table, you will not catch the infection. I am afraid that you are right, there are students at our University who have already caught the AIDS virus, and some of them are already ill, but even if there are, your son will not catch it, if what you say about him is true.'

'Then how did the others catch it?' Mrs Mkhwanazi asked.

'There is only one way to get infected with the AIDS virus', said the Doctor. *It can only happen if the blood of someone who is infected, or the fluids which come from them during sex actually mix with your blood.* For example, if the blood from someone who was carrying the AIDS virus was injected into your body, you would be likely to catch the virus yourself.

'Fortunately, these days, almost all the blood given in transfusions in hospital is first tested for the AIDS virus. If it is found to be contaminated, it is not used at all. The risk of getting AIDS from blood transfusion in hospital is therefore rather small. But remember, Mrs Mkhwanazi, that it is dangerous to accept any injections from unqualified people. The needles used by unqualified people are often not properly cleaned and sterilised, or are used over and over again with different patients without any cleaning at all. These "roadside" injections can and do actually spread diseases, including AIDS. Cuts in the skin made with a razor blade in order to rub in traditional medicine can be dangerous for the same reason.

'A much commoner route of infection is through sex. If a man or woman has sex with someone who is infected with the AIDS virus, they may catch it themselves. Your son might get infected by having sex with a girl he has picked up casually, carelessly, without knowing her well, because that girl might already have caught the infection. If he does not have sex at all with anyone, he is safe. CASUAL SEX KILLS, Mrs Mkhwanazi; see, I have it up as a poster in my office, to remind everyone who comes here about the terrible dangers of casual sex. CASUAL SEX KILLS; that's what you must tell your son.'

'My husband says that it is only men doing wrong things with men who get AIDS. I really don't understand what he means.'

'I'll try to explain. Some men, from something born in them, or through the influence of their friends, have sex feelings only towards other men; sex with women doesn't interest them at all. Paul talks about it in the first chapter of Romans; it is called being "homosexual", and it is rare here, but quite common in some other countries. A homosexual pair of men can have sex together by one of them putting their penis – that's the male organ – right into the other one's anus, that's where the solid waste comes out of the body. That is what some of them do. It's called "anal sex". It's wrong because it's not how God intended us to use our bodies. It causes little scratches and tears in the inside of the anus. So the semen – the sex juice – of one of the

11

men does actually go in through those small scratches and mix with the blood of the other man, and if one of them is infected with the virus then the other one can catch it very easily. Anal sex happens where men are having sex with each other and it does happen in some countries even when one of the partners is a woman. Doing these things doesn't cause AIDS, but it does make it much easier for the AIDS virus to spread.'

'I still don't understand. I'm sure all the people who get AIDS are not doing these strange things.'

'No, you are right. Once the AIDS virus has started to infect the people in a country, a man or woman can catch it by having ordinary normal sex with a partner who has already caught the infection, and most of the people in Africa who are infected with the AIDS virus have caught it in that way. If your son has sex with a girl he meets at University, and that girl has already had sex with some other man, then it is always possible that the girl is already infected, and she might hand it on to your son. If he does not have sex with anyone at all while at University, he is safe.'

'But our Pastor says that sex in marriage is a good thing. My son one day will want to get married. Will he get infected then?'

'It depends who he marries. If he marries a good girl who is still a virgin, who has never had sex with anyone else, and if he himself never has sex until he has it with her, then they are both

YOU CANNOT GET AIDS BY

Mosquito bites	Sharing cups and plates, knives and forks	Living with a parent or relative who has AIDS
Shaking hands or touching people	Having your hair cut	Eating and drinking
Wearing second-hand clothes	Looking after animals	Sitting next to someone who is infected
Sharing a toilet or bath tub	Playing with someone who is infected	Coughing, sneezing or talking
Swimming in a swimming pool or river	Having an injection with a new or clean needle and syringe	

perfectly safe. If he marries a girl about whom he
knows nothing, and then finds out that she has had
many lovers before marrying him, then he might
run into danger. AIDS is serious; I am very glad
you came to talk to me about it. But you need have
no fears for your son so long as you can trust him

13

not to have sex while he is at University. After all, that is not what a University is for!'

'I am sure we can trust him. He is a good boy and very serious about his studies. And we will tell him what you have told me, I'm sure he will listen.'

'There are good pamphlets being put out by the Government as well; make sure he reads them. And don't forget to pray for him. There are always some students at the University who think that sex is what they have come to University for, and a Christian boy like your son has to stand up very firmly against the temptation to join them. He will need your prayers. Encourage him, too, to go to church, and to join the Christian Union at University; the young Christians there can help him to live a decent Christian life better than anyone else can do. Remind your son that CASUAL SEX KILLS; tell him to have no sex until marriage, and then to choose one faithful partner for life, and to keep to her faithfully; that is a total defence against AIDS from sex.'

'Thank you, Doctor; I feel much easier in my mind about him now'.

'There's one other thing I should have asked you,' said the Doctor. 'Do you know what the letters mean – AIDS? Did you know that it is the initials of a set of words?'

'No, I thought it was just a name. What does it mean?'

'It means *Acquired Immune Deficiency Syndrome*. Our body has a natural way of defending itself against disease; it is called the *immune system*, and it normally works all our lives long, helping us to fight off infections, and to get better if we become ill. The AIDS virus attacks this very system, so that a man or woman with AIDS has no defence against illness. After being infected with the AIDS virus, they may go on apparently well for a long time, but then different illnesses will gradually overtake them. They may die of chest problems, or skin problems, or cancer, or anything else; the underlying cause is all the same, it is because they have lost their natural system of defence. AIDS is a very terrible disease. We have set up a special unit here at the hospital, and we are doing all we can to help people with AIDS, but so far there is no cure at all. As Christians we must not forget to pray for those who have AIDS, and for the doctors and nurses caring for them.'

'Thank you, Doctor,' said Mrs Mkhwanazi, 'for sparing me so much of your time. I think I understand a bit better now.'

2

The Doctor had had a busy morning. Now he was feeling very tired and it was nearly time for a break. He said goodbye to his last patient, and he was just rising to his feet to go out to get something to eat when the door swung open yet again, and a young girl hurried into the surgery. He recognised her; she was Phindile, a young nurse who had recently come to work in the town, and who attended the church which the doctor himself attended.

'Good morning,' he said. 'What can I do for you?'

'I'm so sorry,' she said, 'but I'm working, and we are so busy on the ward I couldn't get away before. Could you possibly spare me a few minutes? I'm in such a difficulty I don't know which way to turn, and I need your help, really I do.'

The Doctor looked at his watch, and sat down again at his desk. 'I can spare five minutes,' he said. 'I'm sorry it can't be longer, but I have to get back to the

surgery this afternoon. Now, what's the problem?
Are you sick? I must say you do not look it.'

'No,' she said, 'I'm not sick. In a way I'm happy.
Edred Ngoni has asked me to marry him and my
father has spoken to Edred's father and the
families have agreed on the bride-price. They want
to announce the engagement next Sunday at
church. But I don't want them to. I'm not so sure
about things.'

'Edred Ngoni? That's the Pastor's son, isn't it? The
one who is an engineer? What's the problem? Do
you feel Edred is not the man for you?'

'No, it's not that at all. I think Edred is a wonderful
person, and his father has been so kind, I feel part
of the family already. No, it's just something Edred
said; in fact, we almost quarrelled.'

'What's the problem?'

'Edred said we would need a flat, we could not
manage in a room in his father's house, because we
would need space for a baby. And I said we would
not want a baby until we had had time to settle
down, and until I had finished my training; I still
have one year to do, and I do so want to finish. But
Edred said that once we were married, the Lord
might send us a baby at any time; we mustn't try to
change His will; and he said his Grandmother had
insisted that we should have children straight
away.

'But Doctor, I don't want that; I want to finish my

training and I want Edred and I to have a year or two together before we have children, to settle down together and get to know each other. But Edred says that that is not what God meant for people who marry. Now I don't know what to do. I think sometimes I will just say "No" to Edred; but I love him, and my father would be very angry. Or I think I will say "Yes", and give up my training, and just wait for a baby to be born. But that doesn't seem right either. I really don't know what to do, and I am so unhappy. What do you think? Can you help me at all?'

The Doctor hesitated for a moment. Then he said, 'You are asking me whether I think it would be right for you to use a family planning method for a year or two after your marriage?'

'Yes, that's right,' she said. 'I think we should, but Edred thinks it is wrong, and I am so confused. Can you help us?'

'It takes two people to make a marriage,' said the Doctor. 'I'm sure I can help, but I want you to come to see me again, and I want you to come together, you and Edred. You are a nurse, and you know a lot about these things; Edred is an engineer, and I know he will bring a clear mind to the problem. I feel that if we meet together and have a long frank talk, we shall be able to work something out. I shall be at home on – let me see – next Wednesday evening. I expect my wife will join us; I think it will be a really useful time. Can you manage to persuade him to come?'

'I'll try!' she said.

The following Wednesday evening there they were, Phindile and Edred, sitting in the front room of the Doctor's house, looking rather tense and shy.

'Now,' said the Doctor, 'I would like to start by asking you each a question; it's a question I ask every young couple who come to see me for advice on marriage. Please answer frankly, because it may be a matter of life and death. Edred, have you had sex with anyone at all, before meeting Phindile?'

Edred frowned. 'Of course I have not,' he said. 'I have been brought up well, in the house of my father, and my family do not do such things.'

'Edred,' said the Doctor, 'casual sex is very common in the world today, and because of AIDS, casual sex can kill. It was necessary to ask the question. And Phindile?'

'I can answer for Phindile,' said Edred.

'I think she must answer for herself. What do you say, Phindile?'

Phindile looked down at her hands folded in her lap, and spoke so softly that the Doctor could scarcely hear her reply. 'I have never been close to any man in that way, not even to Edred, and we will not, until we are married.'

'Thank God,' said the Doctor. 'I wish all our young people could say the same. And do you intend, in the sight of God, to be faithful to each other, and to live together as man and wife, one man and one woman, for the whole of your life?'

'Indeed we do,' they said.

'Thank God again,' said the Doctor. 'If you keep to that promise for all your lives, then you are spared one terrible problem, and that is the problem of AIDS. Now that is over, I'm going to ask you a much easier question. Edred, who do you think were the first people to get married in the Bible?'

Edred smiled; he had been taught Bible stories from his childhood. 'Do you mean Adam and Eve?' he said, 'or are you thinking of Abraham and Sarah?'

'Let's start at the beginning,' said the Doctor, 'Let's think about Adam and Eve. Will you open your Bible, Edred, and read Genesis chapter 2, verses 18, 24 and 25?'

So Edred read, with a little smile as he looked at Phindile sitting so quietly beside him.

'Then the Lord God said, "It is not good that the man should be alone; I will make him a helper fit for him, ... Therefore a man leaves his father and his mother and cleaves to his wife, and they become one flesh. And the man and his wife were both naked, and were not ashamed."'

'Thank you,' said the Doctor. 'Now, what do you think is the main purpose of marriage, judging from this passage?'

Edred said, 'Love'; Phindile said, 'Christian fellowship'; the Doctor's wife smiled and added, 'Sticking together even when things go wrong.'

'Yes,' said the Doctor. 'All those things; and are children mentioned?'

'Not here,' said Edred.

'You are right,' said the Doctor. 'In chapter 1 of Genesis it does mention the need to have children so that the human race can survive; children are a gift of God and very important. But here, where God is telling us about the relationship between one man and one woman, His emphasis is on fellowship and love. I think this teaches us that the most important thing in a Christian marriage is love between the partners.'

'I agree,' said Edred.

'The first thing, of course, is to make sure that both partners are sincerely committed to Christ. A Christian must not marry someone who is not living in Christ.'

'I'm sure Edred is,' said Phindile; and Edred smiled and said, 'I first loved Phindile because I could see how much she loved the Lord.'

'Right,' said the Doctor. 'Now notice that they were naked and were not ashamed; there is nothing shameful in bodily love, in sex, in a genuine Christian marriage, and I hope and pray that it will be a joy to you both. If you need any help along those lines, I hope you will come to see me, because pleasure in lovemaking does not come automatically, and advice from a friend can sometimes help a lot.'

'Thank you,' said Edred. 'We will come to see you nearer to the wedding. But Phindile tells me you are concerned about what we think on family planning? What did you want to say to us?'

'I'd like first to know what you think yourself, Edred,' said the Doctor.

'I think we must trust the Lord to know what is best for our lives,' said Edred. 'If it is His will for us to marry, then He must decide how many children we have, and when they come. I have already explained this to Phindile.'

'Tell me this, Edred. When Phindile becomes pregnant, will you let her go to a clinic for advice? Will you let her go to hospital to have her baby?'

'Yes, of course, we will do all that is necessary in that way.'

'Then I think you should also let her go to a clinic to find ways of delaying the first baby until you are settled as a couple and ready to make a home for it. You are a scientist, Edred; you know that medical science can help us to live healthy lives if we use it properly. You know that science has made us able to help women to have healthy children, to breastfeed them successfully, and to bring them up to be healthy adults. A good space between one

23

baby and the next, and a good space after marriage before the first baby is born, is part of the preparation we can make to help to give each baby the best possible start.'

'My grandmother will think our marriage a failure if we do not have a child at once,' said Edred.

'That is a very real problem. Phindile will probably find the same thing; her older relatives will be angry and disappointed and perhaps even try to break the marriage. But remember what it says in Genesis, and remember what our Lord said; a man must leave his father and his mother and cleave to his wife – hold her tight, that's what "cleave" means. You two must hold tight together, showing love to your older relatives but putting each other first. And this is a struggle you have to win. Tell me, Edred; some couples can have no children no matter how many clinics they attend. Suppose Phindile has no children; will you send her away?'

Edred smiled at Phindile and she returned his smile. 'We love each other,' he said. 'We would be very sad, but if that is God's will for us then we will bear it together.'

'Right,' said the Doctor. 'In that case you would certainly have trouble with the older relatives, and you would have to explain to them that your marriage is important to you because you love Phindile; it is not just a way of adding children to the family. It's good to get this straight from the very beginning, and show your relatives that your love for Phindile does not depend on how many children she has! I'd like my wife to tell you something about this problem.'

The Doctor's wife leant forward and smiled at the young couple. 'Did you know,' she said, 'that the Doctor and I have no children? In the first years of our marriage it was a terrible grief to us; we went to many different doctors and we both had treatment of different kinds, but nothing was of any help. We prayed so hard! Then my family told me that God had cursed the marriage and they ordered me to come home; they tried to separate us.

'The Doctor's family were just as bad. We just had to cling tight to each other, we were married, and we were not going to part. Now, years later, we see how being without children has left us more free to do God's will, trying to help other people and having many people coming to our home. Even the senior family members became happy about it in the end. I was so glad to hear you say that you had thought this through, and that you realised your love for each other would not change if you had no children. It is very important.'

'It certainly is,' said the Doctor. 'And if things go the other way, there is a different question. A normal healthy woman living with a man and having sex regularly will remain pregnant or breastfeeding most of the time, and if her health does not break down she may have fourteen or fifteen children. In a polygamous marriage she may return to her people after each pregnancy and get a little rest, but if the two live together, as they should in normal Christian marriage, then that is what can happen. What do you feel about that?'

'That is too many,' said Phindile. 'I have seen these women sometimes in the hospital, and it is very sad; the children are weak, and often many of them die, and the women themselves are very weak too. It is not good.'

'WE HAVE TOO MANY CHILDREN'

'You are right,' said Edred. 'I see what you are saying. If we want a healthy family we should have space between one baby and the next; and for that we must use the scientific methods which God has provided for us, just as we use medicine of other kinds. It is a different way of trusting God. Yes, I think it is right. And I know my parents will understand very well; it is only my grandparents who will object. Thank you, Doctor, I think that is helpful. But I still don't understand how it is to be done; can you help us?'

'Yes, indeed,' said the doctor. 'My wife and I run classes at the Family Planning clinic every week, and a number of young couples come along to those classes, many of them Christians. Perhaps you will join us there?'

Phindile and Edred promised that they would attend.

3

It was a very hot evening, with not a breath of wind
to freshen the air. Even so, the Doctor closed the
windows carefully before he arranged the chairs
for the Family Planning class; the class was held in
a waiting room at the Mission Hospital, people
were moving past in the yard outside all the time,
and he knew that the young people who were going
to attend would not want anyone to overhear what
they were saying. The Doctor's wife helped him to
place the chairs in a circle, and to put a small table
near the Doctor's chair, with a Bible and a few
pamphlets upon it. Just as they were finishing
their preparations, the members of the group
began to arrive. Edred, the young engineer, came
in first; then a young man called Soleman, who was
a science teacher; then his fiancée Rose who was a
secretary; then another young couple and finally
Phindile, the nurse, hurrying in from her work on
the wards.

To open the meeting, the Doctor prayed, asking God to guide them in all their speaking and thinking that evening. Then he looked round at the young people, and smiled.

'I know that this may seem a foolish question, but I want to start from the basic facts of family life. What do a couple have to do if they wish to have a child?'

'They must pray for one,' said Rose.

The Doctor smiled at her. 'Yes, Rose, you are perfectly right, but I did not mean that exactly. That is certainly a good thing to do. But just in ordinary human terms, in scientific terms, what has to happen, in men or in animals, before a child can be produced?'

'There has to be sex between the partners,' said Edred.

'Right. We all understand that. So what is the obvious simple method of avoiding having children?'

'Living together but having no sex,' said Edred.

'Right. If you live with your wife or husband, and never have sex, then there will be no children. This way of living is even mentioned in Scripture; will you please read first Corinthians, chapter 7 and verse 5, Edred?'

Edred found the place, and read from the Good News Version of the Bible. 'Do not deny yourselves to each other, unless you first agree to do so for a while, in order to spend your time in prayer; but then resume normal sex together, so that your lack of self-control will not make you give in to Satan's temptations'.

'What do you think that means, Edred?'

'I think it means that it is possible to live together without having sex for a while, but that if you do it for too long it might in some marriages mean that one of the partners would be tempted to have sex with someone else.'

'Right,' said the Doctor. 'And notice that Paul says, "Do not deny yourselves to each other". I think he assumes that sex is a pleasure and a joy, to both the man and the woman; it is something good which God has given us. Is that right?'

'That's what this Bible verse says,' said Rose. 'But for many women I think that is not true at all. It makes me frightened, Doctor; I sometimes even feel frightened of marrying Soleman. Girls at my office are always talking about men and about sex, when we girls are alone together. Some of them think sex is a big joke, but others of them have had a terrible time, they look so sad, and their husbands beat them, or force them to have sex and have children when they do not want to. Sometimes a father will force a girl to have sex with a rich man for his money. It makes me afraid.'

The group sat very quiet. The Doctor's wife spoke

with tears in her eyes. 'I am so glad you have said that, Rose. It is true. Sex can be used in very horrible ways. But Soleman loves the Lord and he is willing to come here and discuss it all before you get married; I hope your fears will go away, and that you will find that sex in a happy marriage is a very good thing. God bless you, my dear, and God bless all those girls and women who suffer as you describe. And the ones who think it is only a joke are wrong too; it is good for married people to laugh a lot, but sex is better than just a joke.'

'Thank you,' said the Doctor. 'That is helpful, and let's take that as a starting-point. Sex is a good thing made by God. In a happy marriage it should be a pleasure to both partners. Now, what exactly happens when we have sex together? Please do not feel embarrassed when I talk about our sex organs; they are specially important, but they are only organs after all, just like our fingers or our toes. Let's try to talk about them quite openly, so that we can get the facts perfectly straight.

'All men have a sex organ called the *penis*. It is usually soft and small, but when a man thinks about sex, or looks at the lovely body of his wife, his penis may start to become hard. A wife, if she is not too shy, can help her husband by stroking or touching his penis with her fingers; it feels nice for the man, and it also helps the penis to become larger and harder, which is good.

'The wife has an opening between her legs called the *vagina*. It is surrounded by soft flaps of skin

called the *labia*, and in the front of it is a tiny thing
called the *clitoris*. The vagina is usually quite
small and dry, and you can imagine that it hurts
very much if a big penis is pushed roughly into a
small and dry vagina. That is what happens in rape
or in forced sex, and that is what gives rise to so
much fear in many women.

'In happy sex, things are different. The man lies
beside his wife, kisses and embraces her for a long
time – perhaps ten to twenty minutes or more –
before the sex act actually begins. He strokes the
opening of her vagina and the clitoris with his
fingers or with his penis held in his hand. This is
very pleasant for the woman. Her vagina begins to
be slippery and open, and when the man tries to
push his penis into her vagina, it goes in easily. A
little slippery lubricating jelly may help to make
entry easier, especially for newly married couples.
The woman may have to help the man by guiding
the penis with her hand. There is no disgrace in
that for either of them.

A woman often prefers to lie on her back on a
comfortable bed to have sex, with her legs apart,
and with her husband on top of her, perhaps
supporting himself with his elbows on the bed; but
there are other equally useful positions for sex.'

The Doctor paused and looked around. He could tell
from the look on the faces of his audience that they
were feeling rather uncomfortable with the
plainness of his language. He smiled and
continued.

'Once the man has his penis inside the vagina of the woman, a number of backward and forward movements will give him a rush of very warm feelings known as an *orgasm*, and a spurt of liquid will come out from the end of the man's penis into the vagina. This is the *semen*. It is a whitish fluid which contains many millions of the tiny male "seeds" or *sperm* which fertilise the female egg-cells in the tubes leading to the womb of the woman.

'The release of the semen may help the woman also to have a rush of warm feelings, that is orgasm, but it is quite common for the woman's orgasm to come earlier or later as the husband again strokes the clitoris. If the husband is gentle and patient, his wife can enjoy sex tremendously. If a couple never have any pleasure in sex at all, they should discuss the problem together, and also with a marriage counsellor. Paul seemed to think that sex should be a pleasure, and I think we all agree. With a little effort and patience, sex can indeed be a pleasure for both the husband and wife.'
'But I don't believe that pleasure is the main purpose of sex,' Soleman said. 'I think sex is meant to produce children.'

'In this passage in Genesis and in the passage where Adam meets Eve children are not mentioned. But of course, you are right. One purpose of sex is to produce children. Let's think about that. To get the story straight, we have to go back to the woman.

'Every woman has two special female organs called *ovaries*, one on each side, low down in her abdomen; each ovary has a tube near it which opens into the womb which is quite a small organ unless the woman is pregnant. The womb itself opens into the vagina. Once every twenty-eight days or so, one of the ovaries will produce a little egg-cell. If the woman is not having sex at that time, the egg-cell will slide slowly along its tube to the womb, and then into the vagina and out of the body, accompanied by some blood and slippery juice from the wall of the womb. When this happens, the woman is said to be having her period or menstruating. Because of this a woman has to wear a pad of some kind for a time each month to keep herself clean and comfortable.

'Now let's go back to the couple just after they have had sex together. The semen flows out into the woman's vagina. All those millions of tiny sperms swim up the vagina, and some enter the womb. Then they find their way – isn't it wonderful how it all happens? – to one of those two narrow tubes which lead from the womb to the ovaries. The sperm can remain alive up there for several days.

'Now let's suppose that just at that time an egg-cell happens to be sliding slowly down the tube, on its way to the womb and the vagina. The egg-cell will meet the sperm, and one of the sperm may very well go right inside the egg, and join with it in the special way which we call *fertilisation*. The fertilised egg has now become something which will, given the right conditions, grow into a baby; we say that *conception* has happened. It is one of the biggest miracles in nature! The fertilised cell starts growing and multiplying into a ball of cells. It slips on down the tube, and if all is well it fixes itself to the wall of the womb. From then on it is perfectly safe and warm, being fed by the mother's blood system, until it is big enough to be born as a living human baby nine months later.'

Rose said, 'You make it sound so wonderful; every baby is a miracle, then?'

Phindile smiled. 'I've seen so many babies born,' she said, 'and you get over-worked on the maternity ward, I can tell you; but it is still true, every birth is a miracle. To see a live new baby come into the world, it is wonderful; even when we are very tired, we nurses feel so excited, and so happy!'

'Yes,' said the Doctor. 'It is very wonderful. But notice that conception does not happen unless there is an egg-cell in that tube at the very time when the sperm is also there. So the timing of sex is very important. Some days in the month, sex is very likely to produce a baby, and at other times in the month sex is much less likely to produce a baby. Some couples who want to try to avoid or delay having a baby make the decision to have sex together only at the times when conception is unlikely.

'They work it out like this. They start to count the

days from the beginning of the wife's period. For example, let's say that the wife starts her period regularly, every twenty-eight days. If the first day of bleeding is called day 1, the bleeding usually stops on day 4, or 5, or 6. From the end of bleeding until day 8 it is fairly safe to have sex together, because conception is then unlikely. From day 9 to day 19, inclusive, sex must be avoided if you wish to avoid having a baby, because having sex at that time is more likely to result in the sperm meeting an egg-cell in the tubes, and so becoming fertilised. After day 19 the chance becomes less, and the couple may have sex again, ending on day 8 of the next cycle.'

'That sounds simple,' said Soleman. 'I agree that we need to control the number of children we have, so I think that is the system Rose and I will follow.'

'Unfortunately,' said the Doctor, 'It is not as simple as it sounds. We will discuss this again next week in more detail. But notice that this method of control – some people call it the *calendar rhythm method* – depends upon the wife having a very fixed menstrual cycle, and on her knowing exactly what part of the cycle she is in. If you intend to use it, the first thing, before marriage, is for the bride to keep a diary, recording the date every time she starts her periods, for six months or longer. Then she must sit down and do some calculations. If her period is very regular and always 28 days long, then the calendar rhythm method may work quite well, so long as both husband and wife remember that they must not have sex between nine and nineteen days after the first day of each new period. If her period cycle is a short one, as short perhaps as 25 days, then the days to be avoided are days 6 to 16; if she has a long cycle, of say 32 days, then the days to be avoided are days 13 to 23. And if her period cycle is irregular, going sometimes for 28 days and sometimes for several more, or several less, then the rhythm method may not work well at all, unless they get very skilled advice in working out the safest days on which to have sex.

'And notice too, that any sort of rhythm method means that the couple have to live together for quite long periods without having sex with each other at all. If sex is enjoyable, then this may be very difficult; and it is easy to forget the date, and have sex on a day when conception is likely, without meaning to. So the rhythm method really only works for rather disciplined people, who can keep a diary by the bedside and look at it every night. Then again, Paul says that living without sex is allowable for the purpose of prayer; we each have to decide whether Christians can rightly agree to live without sex for quite a large part of each month, without losing something precious from their marriage. And of course it is absolutely essential that neither partner is tempted to commit adultery.

'I hope that this has given us some ideas to think about. Next week we will discuss rhythm methods in more detail, and see what we can do to make them a little more reliable. We always like to close with a prayer; Edred, would you like to pray for us?'

Edred prayed, asking God to bless each of the new homes soon to be formed; and the young people went out into the night, to make their ways to the various places where they were living.

4

Edred and Phindile, Soleman and Rose, with some of their friends, were meeting again with the Doctor and his wife at the Family Planning clinic. Edred started the meeting by asking a question.

'Since last week,' he said, 'I've been talking to one of the engineers I work with. He is a really good man, and he says that his church teaches that family planning is only right if we do it by avoiding sex on the fertile days, and that any other method is wicked. And he says that we must go to a course to learn how to do it properly.'

'I'm glad you have been talking to friends about these problems,' said the Doctor. 'Some churches do teach that family planning is wrong unless you use the rhythm method, just as your friend said. But many other Christians feel that other methods of family planning are also good, and that is my view too; I think there are many possible and good methods, not just one. I agree with your friend, though, that if we do want to use the rhythm method, then we must use it correctly. Churches which recommend it, and Family Life clinics, sometimes run courses on it; if you seriously want to use that method, it would be a good idea to join one of their courses.'

'I took notes at last week's meeting,' said Soleman. 'You said if we want to avoid having a baby straight away after marriage we must avoid having sex between the ninth and the nineteenth day after the start of the wife's menstrual period. It sounds quite simple to me; what is there more to learn?'

'There is a lot more to learn,' said the Doctor. 'Those day numbers I gave you are only roughly right, for a marriage where the wife has a menstrual cycle – a period cycle – of exactly 28 days, and remember that I also told you that some women have a shorter cycle and some have a longer one. The day numbers vary with the length of the cycle. If you go to a course teaching this method, they will help you and Rose to keep records of her menstrual cycle, and to do the sums correctly. They will also tell you details of a different method of finding the safe days. It is called *Sympto-Thermal Family Planning*, or *Scientific Natural Family Planning*, and it should help you to make certain that your dates for avoiding sex are the right ones.'

'Can you explain that method to us now?' said Soleman. 'If it is scientific, then it should be good.'

'I don't think it is really any more scientific than any of the other methods,' said the Doctor. 'That is just the name they have given it. But I'll try to explain it, and you can judge for yourself. You remember I told you that the woman's body produces a new egg once each menstrual cycle? The process is called 'egg making' or *ovulation*. The new egg is produced about fourteen days before the next menstrual period – that's the bleeding from the vagina which we call 'menstruation' – is due to start. The egg is made right inside the body, out of sight, and so it is not easy to know just when this happens; but some women are aware of it, because in the days leading up to ovulation they get a small amount of stretchy liquid coming from the vagina. The pants may even be stained with a small amount of pinkish discharge. Some women get a sudden short sharp pain in one side of their lower body at this time; others may feel their breasts prick or tingle a little. If you get these feelings, or 'symptoms', about half-way between one period and the next, you are fortunate, because it makes it easy to tell just when the new egg is made. If you are not certain, you can check the date by keeping an exact record of your body temperature; there is a very small temperature rise, less than half a Centigrade degree, after ovulation, and if you keep very accurate records, taking your temperature with an accurate thermometer every morning, before you get out of bed or have anything to eat or drink, you should be able to notice this tiny rise. It really is not very easy to do; that's why I advise you to join a course on the Sympto-thermal Method, so that you can get help.

'Now, let's imagine that you have done all this, and you have found out that, for you, ovulation happens exactly fourteen days before the start of each menstrual period. All you need to do now is to keep check on your periods, and avoid having sex from the time menstrual bleeding starts, until three days *after* ovulation. From then on until the start of the next menstrual period, you can probably have sex without causing a pregnancy.'

'I don't understand,' said Soleman. 'You said that a pregnancy happens if the egg cell meets a sperm on its way down the narrow tube to the womb; is that right?'

'Yes, that's right.'

'Then wouldn't it be enough if we avoid sex on the day of making a new egg, and a day or two after that? Why is the time without sex so long?'

'It's long,' said the Doctor, 'because sperm are very wonderful little things! A new egg lives for about two days, if it is not fertilised; after that, it dies, and gradually slides down the tube, through the womb and vagina, and out into the open, accompanied by menstrual bleeding. Sperm are different; they are so tiny we can only see them with a microscope, but they can live for maybe four days up there inside the tubes which lead from the ovaries to the womb. So, to make the method safe, we must start to avoid sex five days before the date of ovulation, and that often puts it back into the time of the previous period. The best method is to avoid sex right from the beginning of a menstrual period through to three days after the ovulation date.'

'I think it sounds terribly complicated,' said Rose. 'I don't think I'd ever understand it.'

'Yes, you would,' said Phindile. 'And I could help you; we learnt how to take temperatures carefully, and keep good records in my nursing course. But there is a question I want to ask. If you have an illness, your temperature rises anyway; and if you have an infection in the vagina, you get a discharge in your pants. How can you tell the ovulation date if that sort of thing can happen?'

'You are right, Phindile,' said the Doctor. 'This Scientific Natural Family Planning Method can only work if the wife is in really good health. And even if there is no illness, the record-keeping has to be done very carefully. It is a method which can only be used if both husband and wife are rather careful people, and are both determined to make it work; both of them must remember which days are safe and which are not, and both must be willing not to have sex on the dates when conception of a baby is likely. It won't work at all if the husband, or the wife, is not willing to co-operate. For example, a Christian woman with a husband who drank a lot of beer, and who wanted sex with her each time he was drunk, would be wrong to try to use any sort of rhythm method; it just would not work. As a very different example, imagine a Christian couple who are separated for a while by work or study; when they do manage to meet, it will be difficult for them to think about 'safe' days before making love together.'

'And there is another point I ought to make,' the Doctor continued. 'The rhythm method means no sex for about half of married life. Many couples manage this very well; in fact, they say it makes sex much more precious and worth-while when they are able to have it. They also like the fact that once they have learnt how to follow the method accurately, it is private to them alone; they do not need to go to a clinic or chemist's shop, and no one else need know what they are doing. But going without sex for two weeks or so, even by agreement, might be difficult for some married people. Temptation can come at any time to any one of us. Imagine a couple where the girl has persuaded the man to use the rhythm method. Perhaps he is not really quite convinced, but he is doing it to please his wife. He may stick to it quite well when he is at home; but perhaps when he is away from home, some other woman, a prostitute perhaps, may tempt him, and he may have sex with her, feeling that he is justified because his own wife will not have sex with him at that time. What may happen then?'

'The other girl may get pregnant,' said Rose.

'Yes,' said the Doctor. 'And we all know marriages

which have broken in just this way. But there is another risk; if the girl he goes with has had sex with many other partners, there is a very serious risk that he may catch AIDS, the deadly disease which is spread by sexual contact; and if he does that, he will bring it home with him to his own faithful wife, and may infect her and later her baby. Similarly, a wife on the rhythm method must not be tempted to fill the gap by having sex with other men. The results could be just as terrible.'

'I'm sure none of us would behave like that,' said Soleman, very indignantly.

'No,' said the Doctor, 'I think you would not. But others might, and it is well to think about the dangers. I think that is enough for one evening. Let's pray together before we go.'

5

The Doctor and his wife usually prayed together each week, just before the couples came in for the Family Planning class. They prayed for each of the group members separately, by name, because they realised that each one had his own special needs; Edred the engineer, Phindile the nurse, Soleman the science teacher, Rose the secretary, and the others, each had their own particular way of looking at life, and their own special problems. The Doctor and his wife prayed that each couple would find happiness together in a long-lasting and truly Christian marriage.

One evening, after their prayer-time together, when the Doctor and his wife were getting the room ready for the meeting, the Doctor's wife pointed to a banana the doctor was holding in his hand, and laughed.

'What's that for?' she asked. 'Are you going to give it as a prize to the one who gives the most right answers?'

'No,' replied the Doctor. 'You know I told the class members that we would have to talk about the sex parts of the body just as if they were fingers and toes, without getting shy or embarrassed? Well, its easy to tell young people to do that, but it is really difficult for them to obey! Then I read about a television programme where they used a banana to show how to put a condom onto a penis, and it seemed such a good idea I brought a banana and a condom along to the class. I thought it would help them not to feel embarrassed.'

'I think your banana is a fine idea. Let's see how it goes.'

The members of the class arrived, greeted each other, and sat down. When the Doctor picked up the banana, and asked them to imagine that it was a penis, they laughed a little, but it did seem to help them to relax and not to feel embarrassed, just as the Doctor had hoped.

'We have all agreed,' said the Doctor, 'that during the act of sex, when a man is feeling that rush of warmth and pleasure which we call an orgasm, a special liquid called 'semen' comes spurting out of the very tip of the penis. Normally, this happens when the penis is right inside the girl's body, in her vagina, and so the semen gets right inside there too. Now it's the semen that carries the sperm, the special male cells which are needed to turn a female egg into something which could grow into a baby.

'Now if we pretend that this banana is a man's penis during sex, then the semen with the sperm would come spurting out of the end – here! The man feels good, and his wife will also feel a rush of pleasure. The semen flows into the vagina, the sperm swim through the womb and up those long tubes we talked about, and if there is an egg waiting there ready to be fertilised, it is possible that a baby will be produced.

'Now let's suppose that the couple love each other, and enjoy sex, but that they don't want a baby just yet. They want to wait a little while, to get used to each other, perhaps even to save a little money to give their baby a better start in life. How can the man and the girl have sex together, and yet stop that semen finding its way into the girl's body?'

Soleman spoke slowly and rather reluctantly. 'My relatives are not Christians,' he said. 'In fact, I am the only believer in my family. And I have an old Uncle who has worked away from home, in the mines, for long, long periods, away from his wife. He talks a lot, and he has told me that some men there go with many, many women – no, I don't think it is a good idea, I am just saying what he told me. He said if a man goes with a woman, and he doesn't want to give her a child, he just pulls out his penis before the semen starts to come, so that the semen doesn't go inside the woman's body. He says that in that way he can have sex but get no children. When one of his women had a child, he angrily told her she had been with another man'.

'Thank you,' said the Doctor. 'Yes, it is very sad, but men who are away from their wives for long periods do sometimes behave as your uncle behaved, unless of course they are living very close to Christ and to His pattern for life. It is very wrong, and very sad, for the women, for the man himself, and for his wife at home. Have you tried to witness to your uncle? I expect that now he is old he will be regretting this life he has led.'

'Yes, indeed,' said Soleman. 'We have long talks about it all; I am so sorry for him because he is sad and lonely. But is it true that the method he talks about will really prevent starting a baby?'

'I think I would say,' said the Doctor, 'that it is partly true. The method of pulling out the penis before the semen starts to come is a very old one; it is call *coitus interruptus*, and I am sure Phindile has heard it discussed in lectures. Yes, it does reduce the chance of having a child, and some married couples do try to use it. It is not a good method; I would never recommend it. For one thing, the man loses a little semen before the main flow, and so the woman may get pregnant even though he pulled out early; so it is not at all a safe method. I expect that is what happened to the woman your uncle was sleeping with, Soleman; poor soul, the child may well have been your uncle's after all.

'Again, many men find the pulling out difficult to do; they may get excited, and forget, and then the semen goes into the woman's body and a baby may

52

result. And finally, for many women, this method means that they get no sexual satisfaction at all, because women usually reach their orgasm, their flush of pleasure, later than men do. It's a possibility, but I would not recommend it to any couple who seriously want a happy marriage and a well-spread family. Can you think of any other method?'

'I suppose you are thinking of condoms?' said Phindile.

'Condoms? For Christians?' said Edred. 'I've seen them, but I thought only wicked men used them; the men who have them always seem to be laughing in a silly way, and talking very badly about women. I'd be ashamed even to touch one.'

'Yes,' said the Doctor. 'I did mean condoms. It is true, as you say, Edred, that some people do use them for very bad purposes, but let's forget about that for the moment.

'Many Christians feel that the condom itself is not bad, if it is used in a good and happy marriage, and I agree with them. Let's think what a condom really is. Here is one' – and he tore open a small plastic packet and took out a small circle of rubber with a rolled-up edge. 'Look,' he said. 'This is an unused condom'. Then he picked up the banana. 'Now, imagine that this banana is a hard penis, just before the man and woman make love. The man can take the condom, place it on the end of the penis, and unroll it down the penis, leaving the end loose but pressing out all the air. It should cover the penis completely.'

As he talked, he unrolled the condom to cover the banana, making the young people smile because it looked so ridiculous. The doctor smiled too but went steadily on with his demonstration.

'Notice,' he said, 'that I squeeze the air out of the empty tip of the condom as I unroll it down the penis, so that when it is on it looks like a glove finger which is slightly too long. Now, we will put a smear of this special cream on the outside of the condom to make it slippery. Then the man can go on with the sex act in the ordinary way. When his semen comes out, it will be trapped in the condom; there is plenty of space, because of the empty bit left at the end when the condom was put on.

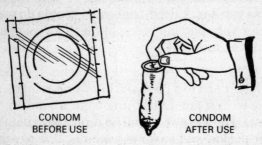

CONDOM
BEFORE USE

CONDOM
AFTER USE

'While the penis is still hard, the man should hold the condom on carefully, and move to separate himself from his wife. Then he can take the condom off, being careful not to spill any semen, and wrap it up and throw it safely away. So long as no semen enters the woman's body, no baby can be produced.

This is a good method if it is used carefully. It stops any contact between the man's semen and the woman's egg; no harm is done; but no baby can be produced.'

'How can we get condoms?' asked Edred. 'I've heard men talking about getting them from drinking clubs in the town, but I would not want to go to places like that for them; my father and his church members would be very angry if I did.'

'There is no need to go to any place you would not normally want to go to,' said the Doctor. 'They can be bought at a chemist's, or at a Family Planning clinic; here, where we are meeting, is the room where they hold the clinic, and in the daytime when the clinic is open you can buy them here in this room. Unfortunately they cost quite a lot; and each condom should not be used more than once. So the method is quite expensive, though a lot less expensive than feeding and clothing and educating a family which is too big for you!'

'And what is that special cream you are using?' said Rose.

'It is a cream which the man should put on the outside of the condom, or the woman should put inside her vagina, before they have sex together,' said the Doctor. 'It will make the condom and the vagina slippery, so that the penis will go in easily. It is best to use a special cream, or jelly, obtained from a Family Planning clinic, which will kill any sperm which happen to leak round the opening in the condom and enter the vagina; it's just an extra precaution. Unfortunately these spermicide creams, or jellies, or vaginal tablets, are also quite expensive. So using the condom method does cost a little money. And condoms are not always perfect; sometimes a condom breaks or leaks during sex so that a pregnancy results. And notice too that, like all family planning methods, this one has to be chosen and decided on by the man and wife themselves; the man has to remember to buy the condoms and his wife has to remind and encourage him to use them regularly, or the method is a failure.'

'That's like all the methods, isn't it,' said Edred. Husband and wife need to work together. I think that is an important lesson we have all learnt from these classes.'

'You are right, Edred. Next week we will discuss some methods which depend on the wife wearing protection, rather than the husband, but the same rule applies; in a marriage, we really cannot achieve much unless we both work at it together. May God bless you all.'

6

The members of the group were encouraged to bring interested friends along with them to the meetings. One evening, Rose brought along her cousin Thandi. Thandi looked thin and weak; Rose introduced her to the other members, and explained that the beautiful baby boy on Thandi's back was her fourth-born.

'And I am tired. I am praying the good Lord God to give me a rest,' said Thandi. 'I have been very sick, and the doctor said it would be good to have no more children for several years. Our house is very small; we have no room for more children. Everybody in our area has problems with finding places in primary school; I know people who have sat up all night long in the cold outside the Headmaster's office, and then in the morning they are told 'No, no place'. My husband is working, but he does not earn a lot of money; and he drinks. I am sorry, but it is so. So I do not get so much of the money for myself and the children. When I am not pregnant I can try to get work, because my mother will look after the children for me while I am working; but when I am pregnant I can do nothing. That is my problem. I talked with Rose, and she said I should come to this meeting.'

'I am so glad you have joined us,' said the Doctor. 'And so glad you have brought your baby with you. What do you call him?'

Thandi smiled, and turned her head over her shoulder towards her baby. 'His name is Mandla,' she said, 'and he is a fine boy.' She slipped him off her back and into her arms, and sat down beside her cousin. Mandla sat on her lap contentedly, smiling round at the company.

'This is good,' said the Doctor, 'because having Mandla here reminds us how precious children are; we long for children, we pray for them and we accept them as a gift from God. That's right, isn't it, Mandla? But we want each child to have a fair chance; enough love, enough to eat, clothes to wear, somewhere comfortable to sleep, a chance of a good education, and a job to go to when he is older. All our countries are struggling to provide this for our children; and in most of our countries we are meeting problems. The clinics are crowded, the hospitals are crowded; it is impossible for all the children of Grade One age to be admitted at school, the schools are already too full so that classes are too large. Even the ones who have gone all through primary school cannot gain a place in secondary school, and even those who have gone through secondary school are often left without a college place or a job to go to; and so we have children on the streets, and problems such as drug-taking and crime. We love our children so much that we long for each and every one to have a happy childhood and a good start in life. Dear little Mandla, your mother is quite right to want a rest, so that she can care for you properly. Tell me, Thandi, what does your husband think about it? Does he want another child quickly?'

'No,' said Thandi. 'My husband is not a Christian – I thought he was when I married him, but I was wrong – but he is a good man in his way, better than most. I think he is afraid that if I go on having children so fast, I will die, and then who will care for my baby and the other children?' She looked down at little Mandla and gave him a hug. 'Rose told me about your talk on condoms; I am sure my husband would not understand, he would not use one, and even if he began to use condoms he would forget to when he was drunk. Life can be very hard for a woman if her husband drinks. I need something I can use myself; and that is why I have come tonight.'

'Good,' said the Doctor. 'There are many other people in your position; and some couples, even if they have no special problem such as yours, agree together that they would rather leave family planning to the wife. There are a number of things which you can do. Let's take them in order.'

Phindile interrupted the Doctor. 'Doctor,' she said, 'baby Mandla is still taking milk from Thandi; see, he is feeding now, look at him! He is such a lovely baby! Does that not stop her getting pregnant?'

'Yes, but not completely,' said the Doctor. 'If Thandi is feeding the baby completely herself, letting him suck whenever he is hungry, and giving him no extras at all, no extra food and no extra milk, then the breastfeeding should prevent eggs being produced, and she should have no periods as long as the breastfeeding lasts. So it should be possible to have sex without risk of a pregnancy. But in practice, the protection is not complete. Many women find that they become pregnant while still feeding a baby, because eggs have begun to be made again before they knew it was happening. Remember that an egg is made two weeks before there is any bleeding from the vagina!'

'The old women in the villages say that if that happens she must stop feeding the baby at once, because her milk will be bad for it,' said Phindile. 'But I know that is not true. They told us on the nursing course that the milk is still perfectly safe for the baby even if the mother is pregnant; she can go on feeding him for a few months, provided she is getting plenty of good food and plenty of water to drink. That gives her a chance to wean the baby onto milk and porridge and other foods, nice and slowly.'

'You are right,' said the Doctor. 'But Thandi

certainly does not look strong enough to carry the double burden of becoming pregnant while she is still feeding Mandla; and for any woman, it is certainly best to leave a good gap between one baby and the next. So we need to talk about ways in which a woman can prevent herself becoming pregnant too soon. And here is something she can use. It is called a *diaphragm*, or *cap*.'

DIAPHRAGM

He took out a small cardboard box, opened it, and showed them a round piece of rubber in the shape of a saucer. The raised rim was thickened and springy; he explained that a steel spring was set round the rim, inside the rubber. He bent the cap between his hands and showed them that it was soft and yet springy. He took some spermicidal cream, and smeared it on the cap. Then he folded each side upwards to make it into the shape of a boat. 'The wife takes this,' he said, 'with the sides curved upwards like that, and slips it into her vagina. It's tricky the first time, but it gets easier with practice, and the cream makes it slippery and easy to insert. She slips her finger in too – make sure it is washed first! – and fits the cap up over the mouth of the womb, which is at the top of the vagina. She should put it in each evening; if sex occurs, then the penis slides under the cap, and the sperm is kept away from the entrance to the womb. It's best to leave it in, after having sex, for at least eight hours. By then there is little chance of the sperm still being able to get into the entrance to the womb and causing a pregnancy.'

'Does it cost a lot?' asked Thandi, 'That is a big problem for us.'

'It costs more than a single condom,' said the Doctor, 'but it will last for a year or more, if you wash it carefully each time, dry it, dust it with talcum powder, and put it away in a box. So it is usually cheaper in the end than using condoms, which should only be used once.'

'And where do you buy the caps?' Rose asked.

'At a Family Planning clinic or a chemist's; but before you buy one, you must go to a doctor, or a nurse trained in family planning, to find which size you need. The cap must fit firmly or it will not do its job. And each time you have a new baby, you are likely to need a new fitting, because the vagina is usually much bigger after a birth. For some people, the Family Planning clinic may recommend a different type of cap, a much smaller one which fits right over the neck of the womb. And then you need to buy the spermicidal cream to use with the cap. Using the cap method does require a bit of thought, and some money, but it is a good method, and many couples use it regularly.'

'I am worried about the cost,' said Thandi.

'I wish I could say that these things are always available free,' said the Doctor. 'But I cannot. I can, though, tell you of something you can do in an emergency, if you are unable to afford a cap just at first. Take a very clean piece of white cloth about six inches square, and fold it and roll it up to form a solid plug about as thick and as long as your thumb. Tie a piece of clean strong thread or thin string round the centre of the plug. Then soak the plug in a cup of warm boiled water, to which you have added either a big spoonful of lemon juice or a big spoonful of vinegar. Or, you can soak it in soap solution, made by dissolving a piece of mild pure soap about the size of a pea, in a cupful of warm water. Or, you can soak it in clean cooking oil, or in melted fat, or butter, or margarine. All these things kill sperm and make the plug safe to use. Then push the soaked plug right up to the top of the vagina; it will cover the mouth of the womb and prevent sperm from getting in. Eight hours after intercourse it must be pulled out, gently, and thrown away. Never try to use a plug twice; you could give yourself an infection by doing that. And do not douche yourself; people used to recommend douching, that is, putting a lot of liquid into the vagina to try to wash out the sperm, as a means of stopping pregnancy. It does not work, and it is also dangerous, as it can put germs up inside the body. My advice is to leave douching alone; it is not a good method at all.'

63

'And how about the Pill?' said Phindile. 'We haven't said anything about that yet.'

'That's so,' said the Doctor. 'Would you like to start, Phindile, and explain to us what the Pill really is?'

Phindile smiled. 'I don't know why it is called "the Pill",' she said, 'because there are lots of pills in medicine. But I suppose this one is special. It is not for people who are ill; it is for people who want to have sex without risk of having a baby. If you want to take the Pill, you should go to see a doctor. He will make sure you are generally healthy, and then he will tell you which sort of Pill to take, because there are many sorts. They usually come in a packet containing a supply for one month, each numbered separately. He may tell you to start on the fifth day after the start of a normal period. Then you take one pill each day at the same time, regularly, without missing a single day, until the pills in the packet are finished. You usually then have a break for seven days with no pill. During these seven days you will have what seems to be a light period, with less bleeding than usual. At the end of the seven days, you start to take the Pill again for the next month. If you are absolutely regular, you will not become pregnant. You should avoid sex or use another family planning method such as the condom for the first two weeks of your very first packet of pills if you started to take them on the fifth day of your period.

'You might be told to start your first packet of pills on the first day of your period; in that case no other precaution is needed. You are protected against pregnancy from the beginning.'

'It sounds wonderful,' Rose said, and then she asked, 'But how does it work?'

The Doctor answered, 'It works by hormones. A hormone is a sort of chemical messenger in the blood which tells your body to change in a certain way; during pregnancy, hormones are put into the blood which cause big changes in the way the body works.

'The Pill itself is a hormone, very similar to the natural ones: it gets into the blood stream and "tells" the body that it is already pregnant. The body is therefore unwilling to make another egg, because it already feels pregnant.

'The Pill works well, but take note that it must be prescribed by a doctor, and it must be taken regularly. Never borrow Pills from a friend, or take just a few, or let anyone borrow yours. The Pill is only useful if it is taken regularly in the proper way. And it is rather expensive, unless you can get it at a reduced price from a clinic, because you have to keep on buying the packets month after month.'

'Isn't it dangerous?' said Rose. 'I've heard of people dying because of the Pill.'

'People die from many things,' said the Doctor, 'including having too many babies. If you go to a doctor first, he will make sure it is safe for you to take the Pill. People who have had certain blood and liver diseases, or high blood pressure, in the past, should not take the Pill, and if women are heavy smokers it is better for them if they choose a different method. But even without the Pill, smoking is dangerous, and I hope none of us here is a smoker.'

'I've heard of an injection,' said Rose, 'just one prick, and it acts like the Pill. Is that done here in this country?'

'They are trying it,' said the Doctor. 'Yes, it is an attractive idea; a woman can go to the hospital and get a single injection, and that will give her body enough of this special hormone to prevent pregnancy for three months. Some Government authorities are happy with these injections, but others are not sure that they are safe, partly because they tend to upset the menstrual cycle.

'And there is another method which we should mention,' said the Doctor. 'It is called the *Loop* or the *IUD*; the letters stand for *intra-uterine device*. Here is one for you to look at.' He opened another small box, and took out what looked like a small hook, made of wire and plastic, with a thread hanging from it. He said, 'If you go to have a loop fitted, the doctor will first examine you carefully to make sure that you are in good health. Then he will take one of these loops, or some other similar design, ready sterilised, and he will slip it right up inside the womb through a narrow tube.'

'Doesn't it hurt?' said Rose.

'It may feel a little bit tight as it goes in but it does not really hurt,' said the Doctor. 'The thread will hang down into the vagina, so that you can feel it with your fingers and be sure the loop is safely in place. Once it is there, there is very little chance that you will become pregnant.'

LOOP

'How long can it stay there?' said Thandi.
'Some of them have to be changed every four or five years,' said the Doctor. 'Others can stay for longer than that. You may have to pay to have the device fitted. But once fitted there is no more money to pay. So the method is quite cheap, and is quite popular. But there are problems. Some women find that wearing a loop gives them heavy bleeding, or pain, and some women seem to catch internal infections more easily if they are wearing a loop. So they do not suit everybody. And there is another point, which a Christian couple will consider very seriously.

'No one quite knows how the loop works, but one theory is that eggs are fertilised up in the tubes near the ovaries in the normal way, and then move down into the womb, but fail to settle in the wall of

67

the womb because the loop has produced changes there. So the fertilised eggs die and pass out through the vagina. This makes some Christians people unhappy; they would prefer a method, such as the condom or the cap, which prevents the sperm ever meeting with the egg at all. It is a matter for the individual couple to decide.'

'Doctor,' said Phindile. 'Could you tell us about sterilisation? Some friends of mine have six children, they do not want to have any more and they are thinking about sterilisation.'

'Thank you,' said the Doctor. 'Yes, I meant to talk about that. If a married couple have agreed together that they will never want to have another baby, under any circumstances, they might consider a permanent method of stopping pregnancy. This is called *sterilisation* either of the husband or of the wife. It is a small operation if it is done on a man. The tubes carrying the sperm are cut or blocked at the top of the testes through a very small cut on each side. It is a bigger operation if it is done on the wife; the tubes carrying the eggs to the womb have to be cut or blocked on both sides through a cut made in the skin of the abdomen. It is done using anaesthetic so it is not painful. Afterwards the man is still a normal healthy man, he produces semen during sex in just the same way as before and his sex feelings are the same, but within a few months of the operation there will be no sperm in his semen so he cannot make his wife pregnant from then on. If a woman is sterilised she is still a normal healthy woman, she still has her womb and her monthly periods, and can still enjoy sex, just as before. But she cannot get pregnant because her eggs cannot be fertilised by sperm or settle into the walls of the womb.

'Many Christians who know their families are complete have chosen this method, but it is only suitable for those who are completely sure that they will *never* want another baby whatever happens.'

The Doctor closed his folder of notes, and looked round the room. 'We have covered a lot of ground this evening,' he said, 'and I hope we have given Thandi some help with her problem. Little Mandla has gone to sleep. He looks very comfortable on Thandi's lap. Let's pray for Mandla and his brother and sisters, and for Thandi and her husband, and for each other, before we separate, and may the Lord guide us in these things as in every part of our lives.' And they all bowed their heads in prayer.

7

The following week, Rose telephoned the Doctor at his surgery at the beginning of the afternoon, several hours before the regular meeting of the group. She was in such distress that the Doctor could hardly hear what she was saying. Finally, she managed to choke back her tears enough to give him her message.

'I can't come to the meeting tonight,' she said. 'My brother Saul is a carpenter at the furniture factory; he came in to see me at the office in the lunch break, to tell me that he was sent to the hospital last week, because his mouth was sore and he was getting thin. The hospital people examined him and found that he had an infection in his mouth. They took some of his blood and did a blood test, and now they have sent for him and told him that he is infected with the AIDS virus; *HIV virus*, the hospital people called it. He has the virus, and he will get AIDS and die. He is my brother, Doctor; my big brother; I am so sad and so ashamed, I just do not know what to do. How can I tell Soleman? He may think we are all a bad family, he may not want to marry me now. And how can I tell my mother and father? Saul is their eldest son, I am only a third daughter; I cannot bear to tell them, and Saul says he is afraid even to go home. What can we do? Oh, what can we do? I am supposed to be working this afternoon, but I have run out to the post office to telephone, and I dare not go back, the people at the office will be so angry with me for going out without permission.'

The Doctor had learnt the art of listening, and at the same time praying quickly to God for guidance. He was praying now.

'Telephone the office,' he said, 'and tell them that you cannot work this afternoon, because your brother is in bad trouble. Then bring him straight round here. I'll see you both before I start my afternoon clinic. After we have had a talk, I hope you will feel able to go home together, and tell your parents the news. And you must not be afraid to tell Soleman; he will be very kind, and anxious to help you all, I am certain. I'll see you soon.'

A short while later, Rose and Saul were sitting in the Doctor's surgery. The Doctor remembered Saul from the past as a well-built young man, confident and talkative, and rather pleased with his own achievements. He looked very different now. He had lost weight; his clothes were crumpled and unbrushed; he sat hunched in his chair as though he were already seriously ill, and he made no effort to greet the Doctor.

'You see how unhappy he is,' said Rose. 'Please, Doctor, do help us; what can we do? What will our parents say?'

Gradually, the Doctor persuaded Saul to tell his story. He was married, and had a child, five years old. He and his wife had quarrelled and separated three years ago. Since the separation, Saul had been living in a single room; he had been spending his evenings in the town, talking to his friends and drinking. At the end of the evening, Saul sometimes took a woman of the streets home with him, and slept with her until the morning. Yes, he had heard about the risk of AIDS; but no, he had not allowed the AIDS risk to make any difference to the way he was living. He was a strong man, and he ate good food; why should he get sick? Then he started to feel ill, and to get thinner. His friends in the office had noticed the sores on his mouth, and they had told the manager; and the manager had said he must go to the hospital. So he went; and at the hospital they had asked him a lot of questions, and had taken a blood sample for testing. Then, this very day, they had sent for him to give him the result. He was infected with the AIDS virus. Now, he said, he knew that he was going to die; he was being punished by his ancestors for all his sins.

'And what advice did the hospital people give you about your way of living?' asked the Doctor.

'Advice!' said Saul. 'I would not stay to listen to any advice. When they gave me the paper from the laboratory, and told me what the words meant, I walked straight out of that place. They had killed me; how could I listen to their advice?'

Rose opened her mouth to speak, but the Doctor looked at her and raised his hand, asking her to keep silent. He waited a few moments, and then spoke again to Saul.

'So what do you think will happen now?' he said.

'Happen? Nothing will happen. I will be disgraced before all the family, and then I shall die.'

'Did you know,' said the Doctor, 'that people who have a positive blood test for AIDS may live for many years, and may feel healthy most of that time? It is even possible that some people with a positive blood test may never get ill at all. You see, when the AIDS virus – a sort of tiny germ – enters your blood, it gradually makes a very small change in the blood itself, and it is this small change which is noticed when the hospital does a test for AIDS. So the test tells you that you have AIDS virus in your blood. It does not necessarily mean that you are actually ill with AIDS.'

Saul looked up, with a glimmer of hope in his eyes. 'Do you mean I might live after all?' he asked. 'Then why do the doctors scare us so badly, if it's all about nothing?'

'It's not nothing,' said the Doctor. 'AIDS is a fatal illness; but the length of time a person can stay alive and healthy with the AIDS virus in his blood depends a lot on the person himself. If you have enough courage and determination to live a good life, helping your body instead of hindering it, then you may perhaps keep well for many years.'

'But I thought that AIDS always kills people? I really don't understand,' Rose said, a puzzled look on her face.

'I'll try to explain,' said the Doctor. 'Let's think first about the normal body. God has provided it with what is called an *immune system*. Your immune system protects your body, just as an army protects a country. If the germs of illness invade your body, the immune system goes into action and fights the germs; you feel ill and feverish while the fight is going on, but when your immune system has won the fight – and it nearly always does – then you feel better again. Is that clear?'

'Yes,' said Rose. 'I think my sister learnt a bit about that in Human Biology lessons when she was at school, and she told me about it.'

'Right,' said the Doctor. 'Now can you imagine a virus – that's a sort of germ – which does not attack the body itself, but which attacks the immune system? The virus spoils the immune system, so that when other germs, or cancer cells, attack the body, the body has no defence. People don't often die of AIDS itself; they die of other diseases, because the AIDS virus stops their body from fighting against disease. It is as if the army of a country were all shut up in their barracks, unable

75

to fight. So when the enemy comes, the country has no defence, and the enemy can walk straight into the country and take control.'

'So Saul has no defence against illness?' said Rose, looking very sadly at her brother.

'Right,' said the Doctor. 'Saul's natural defences are weakened or gone. So, Saul, you must try as hard as you can to keep healthy, because infections are much more dangerous for you than for other people. You must try to live as good a life in every way, as possible.'

'What do you mean, live a good life?' said Saul. 'I only live as other men do, I don't hurt anyone by the way I live.'

'Let's start at that point,' said the Doctor. 'Because you have the AIDS virus in your blood and body, you may very easily hurt people; you may even kill them, without meaning to do it. If you have sex with a girl who is not infected, you may infect her with the virus, and then she will become sick, just as you became sick yourself.'

'Why should I trouble about that?' said Saul. 'Some wicked woman gave AIDS to me; if I give it to another wicked woman, that is only fair.'

Rose could not sit silent any longer. 'Oh Saul!' she cried. 'You know better than that, my dear brother. Even when bad things happen to us, we must not take revenge, or try to hurt other people. Think how sad you would be if some young girl who knows nothing was made ill because of you. No, Doctor, I will take him home, and we will help him to live a better life.'

'I know you will try to help him,' said the Doctor. 'But Saul must make up his own mind about how he should live. Even for your own sake, Saul, you must stop having sex with this woman or that one, just as you feel inclined. You know this moving from woman to woman is an unhappy way to live; it has brought you nothing but illness and sorrow. And these poor women, who have had sex with many men, are likely to have many other diseases, as well as AIDS. If you want to remain healthy you must – you really must – keep right away from sex with them, because these diseases may easily kill you. And, Saul, if you know the names of any you have slept with in the past, you must go to them, tell them what has happened, and warn them to get tested for the AIDS infection. They may have caught it from you, or from some other man, and they will need help, just as you do yourself.'

Saul listened quietly, looking down at the floor.

'Then, Saul,' said the Doctor, 'you will need good food, fresh air, plenty of healthy exercise like walking, or playing games in the open air, and plenty of rest. Smoking and drinking are more dangerous for you than they are for other people; if you wish to live, you must stop smoking, and stop drinking too much beer or other sorts of alcohol. Go home early at night, eat a good supper, and then go to bed; you need plenty of food and plenty of rest.

Carry on with your daily job, you need not worry about infecting other people at work. You cannot spread the infection by working with other people, or by eating with them, or using the same toilet.

'There is no need to tell many people about your illness, but do tell your doctor and your dentist. I'm glad you have told Rose, and me; you will need to talk with us often about how things are going. Your manager may already suspect that you have AIDS, because it was he who sent you to the hospital. If you feel that he should be told, because you are beginning to miss days at work, then ask your doctor to tell him; he can explain the situation to him in confidence, and tell him that it is safe for you to continue to work.

'Do visit your doctor regularly; if you have any illness, get it treated quickly, because it will become worse more rapidly for you than for other people. This sore mouth you are suffering from, for example; that is probably an illness called "thrush", and it can be treated quite easily. Getting that cured will make you feel much better, because it will make you able to eat without pain. Treat other illnesses in the same way; deal with each one as it comes, and keep as fit as possible. And, of course, you must not give blood to the blood transfusion service. Any blood you gave would be tested, and then thrown away, because it would be likely to infect the person who received it.'

Saul by now was sitting with his head bowed. He spoke softly, as if speaking to himself. 'How can I live such a life? How can I go back to an empty room each evening, and wait to die? I'd rather die at once, I'd rather kill myself.'

'It will not be easy for you,' said the Doctor, 'but with God's help, anything is possible. The Bible says that our bodies are temples of the Holy Spirit; if you think of God's Holy Spirit living inside your body, it will be much easier for you to begin to keep it clean and pure. And the Lord Jesus will help you. Whenever anyone comes to the Lord, no matter how good or how bad they have been, they have to get rid of their old life, and start a new life in Christ. That's what Jesus meant when He said, "You must be born again". Being born again means to get a fresh start in life, just as if we were little children'.

'God knows I'd make a fresh start if I could,' said Saul. 'I'd like to wipe out the last few years, and all the terrible things I have done. And there's my wife; I treated her so badly. She was a Christian, and she tried to help me, but I had begun drinking with men from the factory, and going to the town at night, and I wouldn't stop. Then when she shouted at me, I beat her, and the child too; and then I sent her back to her parents, and gave up the home, and started to live my own life. And look what it's led me to.'

Rose took her brother's hand. 'Saul,' she said, 'my

mother and I visit your wife often, almost every week, and we see her often at church. She is well, and the child too. I think if you went and told her you were truly sorry, and that you wanted to come back to the Lord, and to come back to her, she might be willing to help you. She is a very kind girl, and very forgiving, because she loves Jesus, she really does.'

'I know she does,' said Saul, 'and I love her; in spite of the dreadful things I've done, I love her dearly. But I could never go back to her now. How could I bring this sickness on her and the child?'

'That is a great problem,' said the Doctor. 'I would advise you to go forward very slowly. First, Saul, make peace with your parents; tell them what has happened, ask their forgiveness for the past, and ask them to help you. Then make peace with your God. Spend time with Christian people, and spend time reading the Bible, and let God's voice speak to you. Jesus Christ died to save us from all our sins; no matter what we have done, He can move in and make us new. He might even do a miracle of healing, and save you from AIDS; He will certainly be able to do an even more wonderful miracle, and build you up in Him so that you are no longer afraid. If you are born again in Christ, you are a new person, and you can then perhaps approach your wife, and ask her to forgive you for all the suffering your sins have caused her.'

'But the sickness?' said Saul.

'If you do succeed in coming together again, it would be best to have no sex in your marriage. If you do both decide you want to have sex, then it can be made less dangerous for your wife by using condoms, but you must be very careful indeed; you must use a condom every time, with spermicidal cream, without a single exception, and you must take care that not a single drop of semen from your body touches your partner's vagina. It will not be easy, but it can be done. Remember, it must be condoms – no other birth control method will do. And you must have no more children. Children of infected parents are likely to be born with the AIDS infection themselves, and they die very soon. And in making your wife pregnant you are likely to give her the infection; pregnancy brings the AIDS disease on faster, so she might rapidly become ill. These terrible things must be avoided at all costs.'

Saul sat for a moment with his hands over his eyes. Then he lifted his head and looked at Rose. 'Thank you for bringing me here,' he said. 'It all looks just a little bit better than it did. I've got an aim in life now; I want to be reconciled with God, and with my parents, and with my wife and child, and I want to earn some money, in the time left to me, so that I can leave them something to help them when I am gone. If only I could live these years over again! I'd act so differently. But I can't, and the time has gone by. Please pray for me.'

'I'll pray for you all,' said the Doctor. 'Just now you are passing through the Valley of the Shadow of

Death, but remember that the Lord has promised to be with us there, to protect and comfort us. We never need go through that Valley alone, because He will always be with us if we ask for His company. May the Lord bless and guide you as you go to your parent's home; goodbye.'

And Rose and Saul went out of the room together, to face their difficult task.

8

The rain had been falling quite heavily for over an hour. Now it was quite late. Just as the Doctor and his wife were preparing to go to bed, they were startled by a knock at the front door.

'Who's there?' called the Doctor.

'It's me,' came the reply. 'It's Jonas Malinga; I know it's late, but I feel I have to talk to someone. Can I come in?'

Before the voice had finished speaking, the door was wide open, and the Doctor was welcoming his friend with open arms, and helping him to take off his dripping coat. Jonas Malinga, one of the senior Elders of the big city church which the Doctor and his wife attended, was a frequent and welcome visitor at the Doctor's home; but why had he come so late, and in such distress?

The two men went into the Doctor's study, while the Doctor's wife hurried off to prepare a meal.

Mr Malinga sat on a chair by the table, and put his head in his hands.

'Would you like to tell me about it?' asked the Doctor. 'I can see that you are in trouble, my friend; can we help in any way?'

'It's these AIDS funerals,' said Mr Malinga; 'these terrible funerals. I've just come from the Phiris' home; their daughter Dorcas died three days ago. Dorcas! That lovely girl! Just think of it! She grew up in the church, she came to Sunday school and to the youth club, and she was received into church membership six years ago. Soon after that there was a boy-friend the parents did not like, and a big quarrel, and she left home. Since then, who knows where she has been, or what she has done? And when she came back to her home two months ago, she was already dying. A girl of twenty-two, dying.

'My old friend, what is happening to us? Has God deserted us? Does He not love us? How can we bear such suffering? I looked in the eyes of the father, and I felt I had no comfort to give him, because I myself could not see God in this thing. I came to you, my friend, for help; an Elder is supposed to have help to give to everyone, but sometimes the well runs dry, and we need help ourselves.'

The Doctor said, 'Before we start to talk, let's pray together quietly for a moment'; and when his wife came in with the loaded tray, the two men were sitting, heads bowed and eyes closed. She placed the tray on the table and sat down quietly, to join them in their prayers.

Afterwards, the friends ate and drank, and were able to talk together more rationally. They agreed together that Christians shared in the suffering of the whole world; when the world suffers, Christians suffer with it. Then they thought of the times of the great plagues, when many rich people ran away to safer places, while many Christian priests and ministers stayed to help the sick and dying. In times of great trouble, they agreed that it is specially important for the Christian Church to stand out clearly with its message of hope.

'But when the daughter of a church member dies of AIDS, surely there is disgrace rather than hope,' said Mr Malinga.

'The disgrace was in her running away from home,' said the Doctor. 'And perhaps in the bad relationships between her and her parents which must have come before that. But there is no disgrace in the illness itself. It is possible for a man or woman of very evil life to avoid catching AIDS, and it is possible for a person who has done no wrong – a child, say, born to a father or mother who has AIDS – to be born with the disease, and to suffer and to die for sins not his own. My friend, in these terrible times it must be the love of God which we preach, the love which came down to Calvary to suffer with sinful men, and not the judgment. The world can see the human consequences of sexual sins only too clearly; the Church must show God's love to all who are suffering.'

'It is so hard,' said Mr Malinga. 'I know with my mind that God loves our people, and I can say it with my lips, and I can read it from the Bible. But what the people themselves see so clearly is His judgment, killing their child for her sins. Oh God, please help us, please show us how to show Your love in these terrible times.'

'How did she come home?' asked the Doctor. 'Was she still angry with her parents, and still defiant, or was she open to their love?'

'I wish you had seen her!' said Mr Malinga. 'She was very weak, and very thin, but her face was as it had been when she was a little child. She came back to them as the Prodigal Son came back. She came back home repentant, knowing she was going to die.'

'Then,' said the Doctor, 'even in this sorrow we can see some joy. When the parents die themselves, they will see their daughter again. The loving forgiveness of God has taken her to Himself.

'My dear friend, do not be discouraged. The Christian Church is always called to be a shining light in dark places, and the darker the surroundings the brighter must the light shine. We can say loud and clear that God loves all men and all women; that He is ready to forgive and bless everybody, whether or not they have AIDS. We can give warnings about the type of behaviour which makes it more likely that a man or woman will catch AIDS, just as we warn against the dangers of drinking, or smoking, or driving too fast in a car. But when the disaster has happened, when the man or woman is dying of AIDS, we must not point a finger and say, "This is a judgment from God!" Instead, we must remind them of God's cleansing power, of how their remaining years or months or days can be blessed and glorified by the love of God, and of how heaven lies before them if they accept Christ as their Saviour. Yes, my friend, there will be many in that glorious land who have come there because of AIDS, saved and washed clean by His blood, just as we are ourselves.'

'And what do we say to the unrepentant?' said Mr Malinga. 'Dorcas came home so softly, like a dove flying to its nest. But others come home raging, cursing God, cursing all those who have not caught the disease. They are evil, my friend; almost as if they were possessed by demons.'

'If men do not repent, there is little the Church can do to help them,' said the Doctor. 'But as individuals, we can still try to show the love of Christ to such men, to try to soften their hard hearts. And we must not forget that AIDS itself can damage the brain. This terrible anger may be the result of the sickness itself. Only God can tell. Perhaps our churches should offer church members as voluntary staff, on a rota, to help in the clinics where AIDS sufferers are received for their last days. Who knows, the faithful witness of a Christian man or woman might touch even the most violent sinner, and bring him in his heart to the foot of the Cross. The thief on the cross was a wicked man, and he was saved as he died; and this can still happen today.'

'You are comforting me,' said Mr Malinga. 'And I will share with you one good thought which came to me from the Lord, even as I wept with the Phiri family this afternoon. I thought of the children in our Sunday schools. We teach them the words of Scripture, and we teach them prayers and hymns; by the time they leave the school, they know enough of the words of life to bring them to Christ, even if they have not accepted Him already. The words are there, in their memories. When sickness strikes, when they are ill or dying, perhaps far away from home, those words can come back to them, to comfort them and bring them to Christ in repentance. This whole problem has made me very certain that our Sunday school work is desperately important.'

'You are right,' said the Doctor. 'We cannot speak of Christ at every deathbed; but we can try to ensure that all those who come within the influence of the church do hear and know the words of the Gospel, both for their own salvation and for the salvation of others. Who knows when that knowledge may be needed? We are living in dangerous times, my friend.'

'And there is another way in which the church can help,' the Doctor went on. 'We can warn and teach and preach that if young people live clean sexual lives, having sex only with their marriage partners, they are much less likely to catch AIDS. We cannot force young people outside the church to live as Christians should, but at least we can point out the problems and the dangers, and help them if they come to us asking how they should live, and asking how to find power to live as they should. We must make sure that our church members know what answers to give, when they are questioned about AIDS by people outside the church.'

'I think you are already running a young people's group studying these questions?' said Mr Malinga.

'Yes,' said the Doctor. 'We have been thinking about family planning, and also about AIDS; the two are closely related. Some of the young people have even decided to postpone having their own families for a while, so that they can give service at this serious time.

'There is Edred, for example, the Minister's son, and his young wife Phindile. They are newly married, and before their marriage they came to the decision to delay their first child until Phindile had finished her training. She still has a month or two to go before her training is completely finished; but already they have decided to delay their own family still further. I am telling you no secret, dear Elder; the young couple testified to their decision in front of the whole Youth Club, only last Saturday. Phindile has shown great promise as a nurse, and she has volunteered to take the position of Charge Nurse in the new special hospital for AIDS sufferers, which is being opened a short way North of the town. Some people are frightened even to visit relatives there, but Phindile knows that if she takes all the proper precautions, there is no danger. She has given herself to God for this work. There will be little children in that hospital, as well as men and women; think what Phindile's love and courage will mean to them! How could she do such work, if they had decided to have a child of their own immediately after marriage? We can be very proud of Phindile, and of Edred for supporting and encouraging her.

'Then consider young Soleman, and his young wife Rose. They are married now, and very happy together, and Rose is pregnant with their first child. They are so happy! But once this baby is born, they have said publicly that they have decided to wait several years before trying to have another one. The reason is that they feel a great responsibility towards the little daughter of Rose's brother Saul. Saul has come back into the family, but he is already very sick with AIDS. He is most anxious to go on working, but soon it is likely that he will be unable to continue, and then his wife will have to work, to support her sick husband. So Soleman and Rose have decided to open their home and take in Saul's little girl as if she were their own. It is happening in several families; healthy Christian parents are opening their hearts and homes to the children of their sick or dying relatives.'

'Healthy Christian parents?' said Mr Malinga. 'You speak as though Christians do not get AIDS.'

'Christians can catch all diseases just as non-Christians do, except when God miraculously intervenes; and such miracles do happen at times. I have seen it with my own eyes. But the number of Christians catching AIDS will be low, so long as Christians keep to a strict code of behaviour. If our young people do not have sex with anyone at all except their own partners in marriage, then they are almost entirely safe.'

'That is some comfort,' said Mr Malinga. 'But my heart is still heavy. We who know Christ carry a heavy responsibility in these worrying times.'

'Yes, indeed we do,' said the Doctor. 'But it is when the burdens are heaviest that our Lord gives us most freely of His joy. Remember Paul the apostle, singing in prison, and writing to his friends outside reminding them to rejoice! We have the same power for joy which was given to him, because we have the same Lord. We must make sure that the church glows with truth and love and joy, shining like a beacon of hope to everyone around. Let me read to you a scripture which has been a great support to me, and which will, I am sure, support us all until these difficult days are over.'

And he opened his Bible at Romans chapter 8, and read those words which have comforted Christians through all sorts of troubles and problems, in all countries where the Gospel is preached and known.

'What then shall we say to this? If God is for us, who
is against us?

'No, in all these things we are more than
conquerors through Him who loved us. For I am
sure that neither death, nor life, nor angels, nor
principalities, nor things present, nor things to
come, nor powers, nor height, nor depth, nor
anything else in all creation, will be able to
separate us from the love of God in Christ Jesus our
Lord.'

And the friends said, 'Amen'.

FOR LOVE OF FLORENCE
Dr. Kenneth L. Okello

Jackson Labeja and Florence Mugisha, two young undergraduates, meet and fall in love. Unfortunately, they are from different tribes.

Would their parents consent to their marriage? Find out from this exciting novel.

Illustrated 96 pages £1.20
(Europe and USA £1.50)

THE HEALING OF THE SICK LAND
Rev. L. W. M. Xozwa

What should be the Christian's attitude to the frightful conditions of many of the big cities in Africa with their poverty, slums, crime and immorality? The author proclaims in this book that the task of seeking healing for the sick land is the responsibility of Christians, those who are called by God's name.

This prophetic book has an answer for the Christian who is concerned about the healing of the sick land.

24 pages 90p
(Europe and USA £1.20)

THE SECRET OF WISDOM
Derek Kidner

The ancient Wisdom books of the Old Testament
wrestle with questions modern man is always asking.
Does life have meaning? Does suffering have a purpose?
Is a good life possible in the kind of world we live in?

In this book, the author explores the concept of Wisdom
in its near-eastern setting. He examines each of the
three Wisdom books (Proverbs, Job and Ecclesiastes) in
detail. He compares, contrasts and integrates the
teaching of the three books on the subject of Wisdom.

96 pages £1.20
(Not available in Europe and the USA)

GUERRILLA FOR CHRIST
Salu Daka Ndebele (with Dan Wooding)

Salu Daka Ndebele is a Zimbabwean working in a drug
rehabilitation centre in the People's Republic of
Mozambique. He is arrested for distributing Bibles
during a campaign against the Church and
missionaries. While under interrogation, a great deal of
pressure is put on him to join the guerrillas. He refuses
and is imprisoned...

Would he rot in prison for forty years...or change his
stand?

125 pages £1.20
(Europe and USA £1.80)

HELLO GOD
Joseph Aryee

This is a book of simple prayers the child can be taught to say every day. It will provide material to help the child begin to form simple prayers of his own.

DISCOVERING GOD'S CREATION

Joseph Aryee

This book teaches the child about some of God's creatures. It explores the innocent musings of a child about who created all the wonderful creatures we see around us. The answer provided is God did. It has an easy rhyme which can be committed to memory.

BYANG KATO: AMBASSADOR FOR CHRIST
Sophie de la Haye

Byang Kato was born in Northern Nigeria. He attended the ECWA Bible College, Igbaja, studied at the London Bible College, England, and was awarded the University of London B.D. He received the S.T. with Honours and his Th.D from Dallas Theological Seminary.

Although Byang Kato died by drowning at the age of thirty-nine, he accomplished much from the day he dedicated his life to Jesus Christ in 1953. At the same time of his death, he was serving as the General Secretary of the Association of Evangelicals of Africa and Madagascar (AEAM).

Illustrated 126 pages £1.60
(Europe and USA £2.50)